Move & Learn

Early Concepts

BY BETH LIPTON

SCHOLASTIC
PROFESSIONAL BOOKS

NEW YORK • TORONTO • LONDON • AUCKLAND • SYDNEY
MEXICO CITY • NEW DELHI • HONG KONG • BUENOS AIRES

Many heartfelt cheers and thanks to the wonderful children of Davidson Day School
and the thousands over the past eighteen years who have joined me in experiencing
joy and learning through movement and thematic play.

—BETH LIPTON

Cover design by **Jason Robinson** based on a design by Susan Kass
Cover and interior artwork by **Cary Pillo**
Interior design by **Holly Grundon**
Interior photographs by **Julia Pollex**

ISBN: 0-439-21568-4

1 2 3 4 5 6 7 8 9 10   40   09 08 07 06 05 04 03

CONTENTS

About This Book 4

Introduction 5

ACTIVITIES	SKILLS	PAGE
Show-and-Share Opposites	Opposites	8
Letter Look-Alikes	Alphabet	11
One Frog Hopping	Numbers & Counting	14
Going Places	Transportation & Vehicles	17
Busy, Busy Town	Neighborhood & Community	20
See-and-Make Shapes	Shape Names & Attributes	23
Harvests Long Ago	Seasons: Autumn	26
Catching Snowflakes	Seasons: Winter	29
A Sign of Spring	Seasons: Spring	32
Beach Adventure	Seasons: Summer	35
Imagination Sensation	Five Senses	38
From Head to Toe	Human Body	42
Catch the Feeling	Feelings	44
Becoming a Butterfly	Life Cycles	47
On the Farm	Farm Life	50
Dino Dig	Dinosaurs	52
Animal Adventures	Baby Animals & Pet Care	55
Pumpkin Patch	Plants	57
Waddle and Nod	Penguins	60
Sun, Moon, & Stars	Day & Night, Space	62

About This Book

The activities in this book are designed to support prekindergarten through first-grade curriculums through movement and dramatic play. Each activity teaches an important early concept while connecting to favorite themes taught in many early childhood classrooms. By using these activities with children, you will help them use their bodies and imagination to build essential skills and awareness of basic concepts, such as:

- ◆ alphabet recognition

- ◆ numbers and counting

- ◆ opposites

- ◆ weather and seasons

- ◆ shapes

- ◆ the five senses

- ◆ and many more

The activities in this book were developed and tested at Davidson Day School. They are intended to help you put developmentally appropriate programs into practice and to help children use the mind-body connection to enhance learning.

Introduction

Kinesthetic learning—the process of learning through physical movement—is an invaluable method for teaching early concepts to young children. Movement activities address children's need to "get the wiggles out," learn through their senses, and use their imagination through creative play. These age-appropriate activities also offer teachers an opportunity to get to know their students in a new way and to address individual needs and learning styles.

Meeting the Needs of Young Learners

Children learn about themselves and the world around them through physical exploration. As preschool and elementary teachers know, very young children are constantly in motion as they toddle, squirm, and bound their way into new discoveries about their own bodies and the fascinating environment that surrounds them. The activities in this book build on children's natural curiosity and allow children to use their need for physical movement in a constructive and rewarding way.

The concrete nature of physical movement provides an excellent way to teach the abstract concepts involved in children's early literacy, science, and math learning. What better way to learn the attributes of a shape or a letter than by making it with one's own body? Movement activities are also invaluable for teaching children with special needs. Children who have difficulty using language can benefit tremendously from using their bodies to express their learning.

Finally, kinesthetic learning is essential for young children's sensory-motor and socio-emotional development. Guided movement activities help children develop a sense of self-awareness about what their bodies can do, as well as foster an awareness of others. Peer interactions build children's cooperation skills and give them a sense of belonging and contributing to the group as a whole.

Making the Most of the Activities

The activities in this book are designed to fit easily into your existing preschool or elementary curriculum. You will find that these lessons naturally incorporate many curricular areas, including language and literacy, social studies, science, and math. The lessons are organized thematically, so you can see at a glance the activities that will support your units of study. For example, if you are doing a unit on animals you might try "Animal Adventures." For an activity on life cycles, turn to "Becoming a Butterfly." By weaving these activities into your existing program, you can add a physical dimension to your curriculum that is guaranteed to enrich children's learning experiences.

Looking at the Lesson

Each activity provides you with step-by-step directions to guide children through the lesson, as well as handy tips for classroom management and notes for meeting individual needs. You will also find that each activity includes sample dialogue for teachers. You can use this dialogue as a base from which to work, and to spark your own ideas for how to communicate with children as you guide them through the lesson. To make lesson planning easier, each activity has been organized into the following format.

- **Overview:** Summarizes the activity, allowing you to see at a glance the skills and concepts being taught.

- **Getting Started:** Describes how to introduce the activity to the class, access children's prior knowledge, and warm them up for movement.

- **Moving and Learning:** Provides instructions for leading the movement activity, including examples of language to use and the kinds of responses you can expect from children.

- **Wrapping Up:** Provides guidelines for how to conclude the activity and help children articulate their learning and individual experiences.

- **Following Up:** Offers ideas for extensions and follow-up activities across different curricular areas.

- **Try This!** Provides suggestions for movement extensions and variations on the activity.

- **Book Link:** Provides book suggestions for connecting literature to the activity.

- **Sidebar Tips and Notes:** Offer helpful hints for classroom management and suggestions for helping children get the most out of the activity.

Using the Activities in the Classroom

You will find that these activities work best as a class, although you can also use them in small groups provided you have enough adult supervision in the classroom. You may choose to set aside a special portion of your day for movement, or you can use the activities during circle time as a fun and physical way to start or end the day. Use the following guidelines to help children get the most out of the activities.

◆ Clear a section of the room for children to move in. Introduce and wrap up each activity with children seated in a circle—on the floor or rug is best. The circle formation will allow for maximum peer interaction and will also help you to define the area for movement.

◆ To help children make successful transitions to movement activities, try playing a few notes on an instrument to let them know that it's time to begin. Children can show they are ready to participate by taking a spot in the circle.

◆ As you guide children through the activity, join in! You can model movements for children and maximize their participation by working alongside them.

About the Author

Beth Lipton is an educator in both academics and the arts. In 1988 she founded the Woodstock Youth Theatre, an organization that helps children explore the humanities through the performing arts. She teaches standards-based curriculum in schools, including arts-in-education programs and programs for gifted children. She has extensive experience working with children and other educators in a variety of capacities: as a classroom teacher, resource teacher, elementary team leader, and curriculum coordinator. She brings her practical experience and passion for enriching children's learning to her development of innovative approaches to early childhood education.

Show-and-Share
Opposites

This activity will help you to introduce and teach the concept of opposites while children get out the wiggles and have some fun!

Overview

Children explore the concept of opposites by pretending to hold objects with opposite qualities (little and big, heavy and light, hot and cold, and so on). Then, they move their bodies quickly and slowly, up and down, forward and backward. The activity concludes in a circle, giving each child an opportunity to share what he or she learned with the group.

Getting Started

Explain to children that they will be learning about opposites with an activity that has them use their imagination and their bodies.

Let's learn about opposites and what it means to say something is the opposite of something else. Think about the word hot. *Pretend you are picking up something that is very, very hot: a cup of hot cocoa, a fresh-cooked french fry, a steaming bowl of soup. Go ahead! Pretend to pick up something hot. Be careful not to burn yourself! Is it something yummy to drink or eat? What else could it be?*

Now, let's put the hot object down and pick up something very, very cold: an ice cream cone, an ice cube, a snowflake. What other things are cold to the touch?

Invite children to think about a variety of opposites, such as soft and hard, happy and sad, heavy and light, and so on. For example:

What could you pick up that is very, very heavy? A dinosaur?

How about something light, like a feather?

If you find a child who is having trouble getting started you might offer the imaginary item you are holding. After children have had a chance to explore the qualities of each opposite, help them to summarize what they have learned:

So, we have learned that hot and cold are not alike. They are opposites.

Moving and Learning

Now you're ready to ask children to stand up and move! Tell children that they will be using their whole bodies to show what opposites mean. Lead the class in exploring one idea and its opposite, alternately.

Okay, everybody up! We're still thinking about opposites.

What is the opposite of fast? That's right, slow. Let's make our bodies move slowly.

Now, let's move the opposite of slow: fast. Staying in your spot, move very, very fast. Great! Now let's move very, very slowly, like we're moving in slow motion. Okay, now brush your teeth fast. Oops. Don't forget to put the toothpaste on your toothbrush!

Now brush your teeth very, very slowly!

It's time to stop. We have learned that fast and slow are not alike. They are opposites.

Continue exploring opposites by inviting children to move their bodies backward and forward, make themselves look small and big, and so on.

Wrapping Up

Give each child a moment to share his or her understanding of opposites. Direct children who need help getting started with specific questions, such as: How did you brush your teeth? When you brushed them slowly, were you careful to get each and every tooth? Other children may need help getting focused with a simple question, such as: What was your favorite part of this activity? Picking up something heavy? Moving quickly?

Classroom Management

TIP

You might find children calling out, eager to share their ideas. You can redirect children by assuring them they will have a chance to talk about the experience after the activity.

Following Up

Extend children's learning by following up with a writing activity. Invite children to draw a line down the center of a piece of drawing paper. Help them to write *hot* at the top of one side of the page and *cold* on the other. Encourage children to draw pictures showing examples of these opposites in each column.

Try This!

You can reinforce key vocabulary words by playing a game of "opposites charades." Write pairs of vocabulary words on index cards and place them in a paper bag. Invite partners to choose a card and act out the opposites for the rest of the group to guess.

Help children learn correct vocabulary for opposites with gentle guidance. For example, you might find children calling out "unfull" as the opposite of full. Acknowledge that these responses show understanding of the concept of opposites, despite inaccurate vocabulary. You might say, That's right, and the word for "unfull" is "empty"! Full and empty are opposites!

Is there a child in your class who has difficulty finding the right word, or connecting the word to meaning? He or she might have an expressive language disorder. Movement activities such as this one are wonderful for these children. You can help them find the word they're looking for by showing the movement associated with that word.

Two students demonstrate opposite feelings—happy and sad.

BOOK Link

Invite children to explore the opposites that are part of their everyday activities by reading *A High, Low, Near, Far, Loud, Quiet Story* by Nina Crews (Greenwillow, 1999). Full-color photographs and one-word captions show a young boy and girl expressing opposites over the course of a day (they are loud in the bathtub and quiet while listening to a story; they play with a large dog and watch a small ant). After reading the book, you might take photographs of children's activities in the classroom and invite them to label the pictures to create their own book of opposites.

Letter
Look-Alikes

This activity helps reinforce letter recognition and phonic comprehension.

Overview

After children discuss the sounds a particular letter can make, they're invited to form letters with their bodies in several different ways. Then children work with partners to portray a word that begins with that letter. The activity concludes with the partners showing the class their ideas and a final review of the specific letter and the sounds it can make.

Getting Started

Tell children which letter you will be focusing on. Point out that letter on an alphabet chart or draw it on the chalkboard, and review the sounds that letter can make. Have children write the letter in the air in the following ways.

> Today we're talking about the letter e! Let's write the letter e in the air . . .
>> with one finger, as though it is a pencil
>> with one foot
>> with your head
>> with your elbow
>> with both elbows at once
>> with your nose
>> with your bottom (Kids love this one!)
>
> Everybody up! Now, let's shape the letter e using our whole body.
> Wow, look at all these e's!

After directing the class back to the circle, ask children to name words that begin with the letter e.

> Can anyone think of a word that begins with the letter e? That's right, elephant! Elephant begins with an e, a short e sound. The words egg and elf also begin with e.

> Now, let's try to think of words with a long e sound: ee. That's right, eagle, ear, eat, eel! Each of these words begins with the letter e.

If children name words that begin with a different letter, provide positive reinforcement for their effort to answer. (The word *apple* begins with the short *a*, but apples are delicious, aren't they?) Ultimately you are looking for suggestions that will be fun for children to act out in the next step of the activity. Animal, food, or action words work particularly well. Introduce your own words if children are having trouble (for suggestions, see sidebar at right).

Moving and Learning

Choose two *e* words on which children can focus. Divide the class into partners and tell children that they will be acting out scenes to show the meaning of each *e* word.

We have learned that egg *and* elephant *are two great* e *words. Now we will work in pairs to act out each word.*

First, let's try egg. *Decide which partner will be the egg (the other partner will be the helper).*

What kind of egg will you be? A dinosaur egg, a bird egg, a chicken egg? Or maybe an egg that you eat for breakfast?

Now it's time for the partners to start their helper jobs. Will you help the baby dinosaur break out of its shell? Help the baby bird to fly? Or crack the egg open and make a scrambled-egg breakfast?

Next, let's act out our second word: elephant. *Let the partner who helped in the last scene play the elephant.*

How can you make yourself look like an elephant? Can you move your arms like an elephant's trunk?

Now, partners, how can you help the elephant in this scene? Can you teach the elephant tricks? Lead the elephant on a walk through the jungle? Remember to work together!

You will see many variations as children create letters with their bodies. Some will use their bodies in space, while others will need to use the floor as "paper." You might also notice that the same directionality mistakes occur in children's movements as in their writing, such as a backward *e*. If you choose to correct children, you might try a simple suggestion such as: That's a great *e*, but it is backward. Jump and face the other way to make a forward-facing *e*.

Classroom Management

TIP

If you have a pair that is having trouble working together, model ways for them to resolve the problem. Perhaps both partners get to be eggs. Perhaps they meet in an egg carton! They might even get scrambled together in the same frying pan!

Wrapping Up

Ask children to return to the meeting area to share and revisit what they have learned.

Let's take turns showing how the partners acted out the scenes.

Let's have one team share what they did for the egg scene.

Now, let's have a team show what they did for the elephant scene.

Great scenes, everybody!

When each pair has had a chance to share a scene, have children summarize what they learned by drawing one last *e* in the air and telling what sounds the letter makes.

Following Up

Have children make personal alphabet books in which they draw pictures of what they looked like forming letters with their bodies. Or if you have a camera in the classroom, you might take photos of children forming letters and make a class alphabet book using the photos. Invite children to write an accompanying sentence for each picture.

The letter *f*.

Try This!

This activity is great fun at a more advanced level as well. Instead of using single letters, you can teach sound clusters or word endings. For example, you might focus on *-ness* words, such as sadness, happiness, kindness, and so on. Partners can dramatize a scene about happiness, or portray an act of kindness. The activity can also be used to reinforce basic grammar by focusing on particular types of words. For example, after brainstorming adjectives as a class, partners can choose descriptive words to portray in a scene. The rest of the class can guess what adjective the pair is portraying.

The letter *x*.

BOOK Link

Invite children to find letters in photographs of everyday objects by reading **Alphabet City** by Stephen T. Johnson (Puffin, 1996). This 1996 Caldecott Honor book offers up an extraordinary urban alphabet. Each page is a delight, from A (a construction sawhorse) to Z (a zigzag fire escape).

Note

You can do this activity over and over again, focusing on a different letter each time. If children have trouble thinking of words to act out, you might try the following suggestions to get them started.

A: *alligator*
B: *balloon*
C: *cat*
D: *dinosaur*
E: *elevator*
F: *fish*
G: *gorilla*
H: *hippopotamus*
I: *ice-cream cone*
J: *jump rope*
K: *kite*
L: *lollipop*
M: *magnet*
N: *nap*
O: *octopus*
P: *porcupine*
Q: *queen*
R: *rattlesnake*
S: *sailboat*
T: *teddy bear*
U: *umbrella*
V: *volcano*
W: *whale*
X: *X-ray machine*
Y: *yo-yo*
Z: *zebra*

One Frog
Hopping

This activity helps reinforce numerals and build counting skills.

Overview

In this activity, children work together to act out a story in which numbers are the focus. As you narrate the story, introducing characters, actions, and events in numerical order, children provide the action. Use the story on page 15 to get started and become familiar with the process. You can then use the format to create your own stories as often as you choose to do number review. The activity concludes in a circle, as children review the numbers they used in the story.

Getting Started

Gather children together and explain that they will be doing an activity that will challenge them to count in a new way. First, help children review the numbers 1 through 10.

Can everyone count to 10? Let's practice it together—count along with me. Ready? 1 . . . 2 . . . 3 . . . 4 . . . 5 . . . 6 . . . 7 . . . 8 . . . 9 . . . 10.

Now, let's count to 10 again, this time holding up our fingers to show each number as we count. Very good, everyone.

Today we are going to act out a story. It's a special story that uses the numbers 1 to 10. All of you will have the chance to be in the story. Listen carefully, and be prepared to become lots of different creatures and things!

Explain to children that you will be telling the story and inviting them up to act it out. Decide on an area for the "stage" and have children get ready to move and count!

Moving and Learning

Begin by choosing one volunteer to start the story. Tell children to listen closely for when you call their name to enter the action. As you narrate, emphasize the numbers in the story.

Our story begins with one frog sitting on a rock. Luis, why don't you be our frog? Come on up and sit on a rock. What sound does a frog make? Ribit! That's great! Let's start our story.

Once upon a time, there was 1 frog sitting on a rock. Suddenly, 2 butterflies flew by. Lisa and Kayla, you be our butterflies. Go! Flap those wings! Next, 3 ladybugs came crawling by. Who will be our ladybugs? Okay, Caleb, Jake, and Monique. Crawl past our frog in a line. Good. The ladybugs were looking for food. What do you think they found?

They found 4 breadcrumbs! I need four volunteers to be our breadcrumbs. Ladybugs, can you pretend to gobble them up? Yum!

As you narrate, give children suggestions for how to act out each part with movements. You can also invite children to make their own suggestions, and pause at various points in the story to invite children to guess which number will be featured next. Continue the story by introducing the following events in numerical order.

The frog was hungry, so he waited for 5 flies to buzz by. After he ate, it was time for him to take a nap. He fell asleep and dreamed he was at a frog party, where he saw 6 frogs dancing. Suddenly, it began to rain. The frog was woken up by 7 raindrops splashing down. To stay dry, he found a pile of 8 leaves to hide under. When the rain stopped, 9 children came skipping by. The frog joined the children, and they all went out for 10 ice-cream cones.

They ate their ice cream and were very, very happy. The end!

Wrapping Up

Gather children in a circle to share their favorite parts of the story and review the numbers in order.

Terrific job, everyone . . . give yourselves a great big round of applause! Let's review the numbers that were in our story. Everyone say the numbers out loud with me. We had . . .

1 frog, 2 butterflies, 3 ladybugs, 4 breadcrumbs, 5 flies, 6 dancing frogs, 7 raindrops, 8 leaves, 9 children, and 10 ice-cream cones!

Following Up

Invite children to create books for their number stories. Divide the class into partners and assign each pair a different number. Have the partners work together to illustrate that part of the story. Help children label each page with their number, and encourage them to dictate sentences to go with their illustrations. Bind the pages together and add the book to your classroom library.

Try This!

You can adapt this activity to practice different kinds of counting skills. For instance, you might try a story in which the numbers appear in backward order, or create a story using only odd or even numbers. You might even invite children to help invent a story in which they count by fives or tens.

BOOK Link

Invite children to supply the numbers and narration to the classic wordless **Anno's Counting Book** by Mitsumasa Anno (Harper Trophy, 1986). The beautiful illustrations show increasing numbers of objects on each page as the town grows and the seasons progress. Children will enjoy providing their own story as they discuss each picture.

Going Places

This activity introduces the concept of vehicles, the jobs they do, and how important they are in our lives.

Overview

After brainstorming a list of different kinds of vehicles, children will use their imagination to travel to a special destination, transport goods, and work with partners to fix vehicles in trouble. The activity concludes as children share their experiences and review the ways that vehicles help people every day.

Getting Started

Begin by explaining to children what a vehicle is: a machine that helps people and things get from place to place.

> *What are some different kinds of vehicles? Yes, a car. What other vehicles can you name? How about a truck, a bus, a motorcycle, a van, a train? What kind of vehicle moves through the air? Yes, an airplane!*
>
> *So, vehicles travel from one place to another. Who travels in vehicles? That's right, people! All right, everyone, let's get ready to travel!*

Invite children to think of a place they would like to go in a car, such as the beach, their grandmother's house, or even a favorite restaurant. Then guide them to act out their trip through movement, as follows.

> *Okay, everybody up. It's time to go! First, imagine your very own car. What color is it? Does it have two or four doors? Is it a little car or a big car? Now, reach into your pocket and take out the key. Good! Open the door and climb in. Sit down behind the wheel. It's time to*

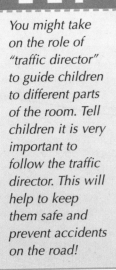

Classroom Management

TIP

You might take on the role of "traffic director" to guide children to different parts of the room. Tell children it is very important to follow the traffic director. This will help to keep them safe and prevent accidents on the road!

start your engines. Turn the key . . . what sound does the car make? Vroom! Okay, now your car is moving. Drive your car to a different part of the room. Put your hands on the steering wheel and turn it as you go. Remember to follow the rules of the road, and watch out for the other cars! All right, everyone, you are getting close to your destination. Start slowing down . . . now stop your car. Open the door and climb out. What do you see around you?

After giving children a moment to explore their destination, direct them back to the circle to share their experiences. You might invite them to bring an imaginary souvenir back from the place they visited, such as a shell from the beach or a cookie from grandma's house.

Moving and Learning

Now it's time to explore the jobs vehicles help people do. Tell children that they will be going on another trip, but this time they will be driving a different type of vehicle to do a special job.

What else can be carried in vehicles besides people? A van might deliver fruit to a store, or a train might carry wood for building new houses. What else might get delivered in a vehicle? Food, clothing, furniture. Great ideas, everyone.

Invite children to choose a delivery they would like to make and the kind of vehicle they might use to transport their goods. If children have trouble coming up with ideas, you might make a few suggestions, such as driving a truck to the supermarket to deliver milk, or driving a van to the florist to deliver flowers. When children have decided on a scenario, invite them to get up and help keep the world moving!

Okay, everybody stand up. It's time to load up your vehicle. Open up the back and put your deliveries inside. Are those boxes heavy? Lift them in—this is hard work! Now, open the side door and get in the driver's seat. Don't forget to fasten your seat belt! Start your engines and go! Move to another part of the room as your drive your vehicle to your delivery stop. Okay, you've arrived. Park your vehicle. Now it's time to unload those boxes! Lift them out, one by one. Great job, everyone!

When children have finished making their deliveries, have them return to the circle. Encourage children to share the jobs they did by asking questions such as: What did you deliver, and to whom? Were they happy to get it? Did you enjoy doing something nice for someone else? Extend the idea of helping others by inviting children to choose a partner to act out the final scenario.

Everyone find a partner. Choose one person to be partner number one.

The other partner is number two. Okay, partner number one. It's time to get on the road again! Get in your car and start driving. Now, something is happening to your car! Maybe it gets stuck in the mud.

Or maybe it runs out of gas. Perhaps a tire goes flat and it needs to be changed. Now, partner number two, your job is to help your partner's vehicle get back up and running! Don't forget to pack your toolbox. Get in your own car and drive to where your partner is stuck. Okay, partners, work together to fix that vehicle. All fixed? Great job!

Now, let's go back to the circle and talk about all the places we went and all the jobs we did today.

A broken-down vehicle.

Wrapping Up

Have children return to the circle and invite them to share the adventures they had with their different vehicles. Conclude the activity by helping children summarize what they learned:

Cars, trucks, planes, trains, vans—these are all different kinds of vehicles. They move people and things from place to place.

Following Up

To help build sorting and classifying skills, invite children to create a transportation mural. On a large sheet of craft paper, encourage children to create a scene that includes land, water, and sky. Then provide children with old magazines and have them cut out pictures of different kinds of vehicles. (Alternatively, children might draw their own vehicles and cut them out.) Encourage children to include pictures of boats, cars, trucks, and airplanes. When the mural is dry, invite children to tell how each vehicle travels—by land, water, or air—and to attach their vehicles to the appropriate part of the scene.

Try This!

Invite children to travel in a whole new way—by taking a trip into outer space! Children can pretend to be astronauts traveling in rocket ships to distant planets. Model how to travel in a different direction—up instead of across—by gradually standing taller and taller as if you are rising through space. Then invite children to get into their rocket ships and blast off! Encourage children to bring something back from their planet to share with the group, such as an exotic plant or animal, or even a new extraterrestrial friend.

If a child is having trouble getting started, you might suggest a place they can drive to, or even ride in the car alongside them. The ice-cream shop is always a favorite destination!

Explore transportation in different cultures and environments by reading **This Is the Way We Go to School: A Book About Children Around the World** by Edith Baer (Scott Foresman, 1992). Children will enjoy the rhyming text as they follow children to school by bus, car, ferry, and even on skis!

Busy, Busy
Town

This activity introduces important social studies concepts as children explore jobs in their community.

Overview

After discussing the roles of various community helpers, children choose a worker they would like to role-play. Then children introduce themselves to the group and show how their community helper works and helps others. The town is then set into motion as children interact and look to one another for service or assistance. After each worker ends his or her day, children return to the circle to discuss the ways in which community members support one another.

Getting Started

Begin by explaining to children what a community is: a place where people live, work, and play. There are many people who help keep a community running smoothly. Help children identify the important jobs community helpers do.

Who delivers the mail? Yes, the mail carrier. Where does the mail carrier work? At the post office. If you were feeling sick, who might help you? That's right, a doctor. If you saw smoke or flames coming from a building, whom would you call for help? Yes, a firefighter. If your pet were sick, whom would you bring it to? The vet. A veterinarian is a doctor for animals.

Today we are going to create our own town right in the classroom. Each of you will have an important job to do in the town.

Help children choose a community worker to role-play. If children have trouble coming up with ideas, you can provide them with suggestions (see sidebar on p. 22). When children have chosen their roles, invite each of them to stand in front of the group and introduce themselves to the class. Then help children practice role-playing interactions by inviting a few members of the group to act out a short scene with each worker, as follows.

So, Andres is our grocery store owner. Andres, is your store open for business? Great! Now, who needs to buy some food today? Lisa and Hector, why don't you get up and go into the grocery store? Andres, can you help Lisa and Hector find the foods they need to buy? Okay, it's time to pay for the groceries. Andres, you can ring up their purchases at the cash register. Lisa and Hector, pay for your groceries. Don't forget to get your change!

Great job, you three. Now it's time for you to sit down so we can meet our next worker.

Continue to rotate workers, giving each child the opportunity to introduce himself or herself and interact with a few classmates in front of the group.

Moving and Learning

Once children are familiar with one another's roles and the jobs they do in the community, it's time to start the workday! Direct children to different parts of the room to begin their work. Remind the group what each area of the classroom represents and what job each worker is doing there. When children are familiar with the town's layout, encourage them to visit the community workers and act out scenarios. To get children started, suggest a few situations for role-play.

I think Meredith may have a cat that is sick. Meredith, why don't you take your cat to the vet to get some medicine? Ben, Donna, and Zach, it's time for school! Your teacher is ready to help you practice your ABC's. Gina, have you gotten your mail today? Why don't you visit the post office?

Continue inviting children to visit various parts of the room. Soon your classroom will be transformed into an active, busy town! Give children plenty of time to explore their jobs and act out a variety of scenarios with the people of the town. Then encourage children to end their workday.

Now it's time for the day to end. I'm going to count to 10. During that time, can you finish your day? Is the vet going to feed the animals before turning out the lights? Does the police officer have reports to write? Does the librarian have books to put away? By the time I'm done counting I need everyone to sit back down in our circle. Ready? 1...2...3...4...5...6...7...8...9...10.

Great work, everyone! Now, let's talk about all the different jobs we did today.

Classroom Management

TIP

In order to give children a full opportunity to explore their jobs and interact with others, have them role-play in shifts. Choose three or four workers to set up their businesses as the rest of the group plays townspeople visiting those businesses. Then have the next small group of workers set up shop as children switch roles. Continue until each child has had a chance to play his or her worker in the busy town; this can be done in succession, or over several days.

Wrapping Up

Gather children together and invite them to share their experiences. To get children started, ask questions such as: What was something you did in our town today that you were proud of? What was something that someone else did that helped you? When children have had a chance to share their ideas, help them to summarize what they learned about the concept of community:

It takes a lot of people to keep a town running! Each person's job is important. And do you know who is a very special part of every town? Children! That's right—and one day, you will be the doctors, teachers, police officers, and firefighters in your own busy town!

Following Up

Invite children to write a group poem about community helpers. On chart paper, list several of the jobs children have learned about. For each job, help children identify a key word to describe what the worker does, and then brainstorm an appropriate rhyme for that word. For example, a doctor's job is to *heal*; the next line might describe how doctors make their patients *feel*. This activity will help children practice language recall based on context, and build phonemic awareness as well. Write the completed poem on chart paper and invite children to create illustrations.

Try This!

Encourage children to act out a quiet busy town by playing a variation on charades. Assign each child a secret job. Then invite children to take turns pantomiming the actions that worker does for the rest of the group. The child who guesses the job correctly takes the next turn. Continue until each child has had a chance to pantomime a job.

BOOK Link

For an interactive reading experience, share **Guess Who?** by Margaret Miller (Greenwillow, 1994). Each spread asks a question about people in the community and provides four silly possibilities: "Who goes to school? Seagulls? Puppies? Umpires? Stuffed animals?" Turn the page, and there is the answer: "Children!" The pattern is repeated for several different questions, such as: "Who cuts your hair?" "Who cleans your teeth?" and so on. Children will enjoy playing this guessing game as they explore the full-color photographs of community workers in action.

See-and-Make
Shapes

This activity helps children identify shapes in the world around them.

Overview

Children discover the attributes of different shapes by identifying examples of various-shaped objects they see in everyday life. They are then invited to create shapes with their bodies and use their imagination to role-play interacting with these shapes (bouncing a round ball, flying a diamond-shaped kite, and so on). The activity concludes with an opportunity for children to share what they learned as they review each shape.

Getting Started

Gather children in a circle and explain that they will be learning about shapes. Invite them to name any shapes they know. To get children started, ask them to identify shapes they see in the classroom, for example:

What shape is the window? A square. What shape is the table? A rectangle. What shape is the group sitting in right now? A circle!

Next, invite children to create circles with their bodies as follows:

Draw a circle in the air with one arm. Draw two circles with both arms. Make a circle shape with your arms. Now try making a circle shape with your whole body. Curl up in a ball. Terrific! Now, let's sit back down and talk about circles.

When children are seated, encourage them to name things in the world around them that are circular, such as the sun, a full moon, an orange, and so on. Then invite children to get up and start moving by asking:

What is something you play with that's round? A ball!

All right, everybody up! Hold a round ball in your hands. Imagine it's a big, round basketball. Try bouncing it on the ground. Great! Now try bouncing a Super Ball. It's a much smaller circle, and it bounces very high. Now choose a partner and play with the ball together. Throw the ball to your partner. Try to catch it! Now throw it back. Try throwing it over your head. How else can you throw the ball?

Give children plenty of time to role-play before gathering them back to the circle. Invite them to share their experiences and describe the different ways they played with the ball.

Moving and Learning

Tell children that they will be using their imagination and their bodies to explore more shapes.

Let's talk about rectangles. How many sides does a rectangle have? Four. Two sides are long, and two sides are short. Look around the room . . . what rectangles do you see? Yes, the door. The chalkboard. The tables. Try drawing a rectangle in the air with your finger. Great! Now, let's think about another rectangle. It's a box—a very special kind of box. It's a box that's buried under the ground. Yes, it's a treasure box! Now it's time for you to dig up your treasure box. Grab a shovel and start digging. Pull that treasure box out of the ground. Hold the treasure box in your hands. Now set it down and lift up the lid. What do you see inside? Bring your box back to the circle and we'll share our treasures.

When each child has had a chance to share his or her treasure with the group, it's time to introduce the next shape.

Let's talk about diamonds. What is something that is shaped like a diamond? Here's a hint: it's something you can fly in the sky. That's right, a kite. Draw the shape of a kite in the air with your finger. Very good. Now, imagine there is a kite sitting in front of you. Pick it up by the string. Ready? Here comes a gentle breeze . . . up, up, up go our kites! Stand up and let your kite fly. Hold on tight! Let out a little more string and fly it higher. Now the wind is dying down . . . let your kite float down to the ground.

Classroom Management

TIP

Keep children focused by participating in the role-playing and by modeling interactions. If a child is having trouble getting involved, you might ask a more active student to seek his or her services, or invite the child to role-play with you.

Wrapping Up

Have children sit back down in a circle. Help them to review the shapes they learned by describing their experiences with each imaginary object. Encourage them to describe what each object looked like and how it felt to hold it in their hands.

Following Up

Invite children to play a game of "shape charades." Divide the class into pairs. Have each pair choose something in the classroom that is a specific shape, for example, a rectangular table. Then have children portray the object without naming it. One partner can become the object while the other partner uses it. For example, one child might get down on all fours as the other child pretends to be doing schoolwork at the table. Encourage the rest of the class to guess the object and name its shape. Continue until each pair has had a chance to portray a shape.

Try This!

Movement and role-play can be used to explore almost any shape. Invite children to think about shapes in new and interesting ways with the following scenarios.

SQUARE: Invite children to build a square television with their bodies. Two partners can create the television shape by standing apart, bending towards each other, and holding hands. Invite a third child to stand inside the television and give the weather report!

TRIANGLE: Invite children to raise the triangular sail on a ship and travel off to a distant land. Encourage them to find souvenirs to bring back to the group. When they return from their trip, invite them to share the special things they found, from exotic fruits to animals and flowers.

OVAL: Encourage children to hold a delicate, oval egg in their hands. Then have them crack the egg and whip up a recipe. They might try scrambled eggs, an omelet, or even add pancake mix to cook up some circular pancakes!

Encourage children to think beyond gold and jewels as they share their treasures. You might suggest different kinds of treasures for children to discover, such as friendship, a sunny day, or food for the hungry. Invite children to use their imagination—they can find almost anything inside their magical treasure box.

BOOK Link To reinforce the concept of shapes in the environment, read *The Shape of Things* by Dayle Ann Dodds (Scott Foresman, 1996). Through simple rhyming text, this colorful book invites children to find shapes in everyday objects such as boats, kites, and houses. After sharing the book with children, you might take a walk around the neighborhood and invite them to point out all the shapes they see.

Harvests
Long Ago

This activity incorporates both science and social studies concepts as children experience the wonders of the fall season.

Overview

After discussing the seasonal changes that take place in autumn, children work together to act out an old-fashioned fall harvest. As they take on the roles of farmers long ago, children learn how various vegetables grow. The activity concludes with an autumn feast and an opportunity for children to share their favorite aspects of the season.

Getting Started

Begin by encouraging children to tell what they know about the fall season. To get children started, explain that fall comes after summer, and is the time when most children begin the school year.

Another word for fall is autumn. *What else happens in autumn? Does it get colder or warmer outside? Yes, it gets colder. What happens to the leaves on the trees in the autumn? That's right, they change color. What are some colors you can see on the trees in autumn? Orange, red, yellow, and brown. What else happens to the leaves? They fall down.*

Tell children that they will be working together to act out a special fall activity: a harvest. Introduce the activity and the concept of a harvest by inviting children to think about long-ago times.

Let's pretend it is long, long ago . . . in the days before supermarkets and malls, before cars and television! How do you think people got their food back then? They grew their food themselves! Fall was a time when they would harvest, or collect, the food they had grown to prepare for the cold winter ahead. Some of the foods they harvested in the fall were corn, potatoes, and onions. We can have our own harvest right here in the classroom.

Invite children to begin the harvest by standing up in a circle. Encourage them to imagine that there is a field of corn in the middle of the circle. Explain that corn grows on tall stalks, and they might have to reach very high to pick it!

Okay, everybody up. It's time to start our harvest! Let's begin with corn. Many ears of corn can grow on one stalk. Everyone start at the bottom of the stalk. Crouch down and grab an ear of corn. Now pull! Great! Now, start working your way up the stalk, pulling the corn as you go. Go higher, higher, higher . . . reach above your head to get that last one! As you pick your corn, place the ears on a pile in the middle of the circle. Let's see if we can make our pile of corn as high as we can reach! Whew! This is hard work! Great job, everyone! Now, let's sit back down and talk about the other foods we will be harvesting today.

Moving and Learning

Explain to children that they will be continuing their harvest with a different food. Next, they will be gathering potatoes, and this will involve different kinds of movements because of the way potatoes grow.

Where do potatoes grow? Potatoes grow under the ground. We're going to have to dig them up. Okay, everyone, let's get on our hands and knees. Pretend to pick up a shovel and hold it by the handle. Now start digging deep in the ground. Be careful as you dig. We need each and every potato! Have you found one? Great! Pull that potato out of the ground. Don't forget to brush the dirt off! Let's make a potato pile here, next to the corn. Look at that pile!

Next, invite children to harvest onions. Explain that onions also grow under the ground, but they have long shoots that grow above the ground. Encourage children to grab on to the shoots and pull until the onions pop out of the ground. Once children have finished harvesting the food, it's time to cook the feast! Guide children in preparing a harvest soup as follows.

Now that we have plenty of corn, potatoes, and onions, let's celebrate with a feast! First, we'll need to build a fire to cook our soup. Everyone pick up some sticks of wood and put them right in the middle of our circle. Great. Next, we need a big pot of water. I need two volunteers to carry the pot to the middle of the circle. Terrific! Now, everyone, it's time to prepare the vegetables. First, we have to shuck the corn. Take off the green parts on the outside and pull the ear of corn out. Now put the corn into the pot. Great job!

Continue by having children peel the onions and clean the potatoes. When all the vegetables have been added, congratulate children on their harvest and invite them to enjoy a delicious, warm bowl of soup!

Classroom Management

TIP

Set the pace and the tone for this activity. As children work, point out that harvesting takes a lot of time. Can they think of something that people might have done long ago to pass the time while they harvested? They sometimes told stories. As they dig, invite children to tell the group a story about something special they might like to find buried under the ground. Perhaps it might be long lost treasure, a beautiful doll, or even an enormous potato!

Wrapping Up

Have children sit in a circle and share what it felt like to work together on their harvest. Did the work go faster with everyone pitching in? What was their favorite vegetable? When children have had a chance to discuss their experiences, invite them to review what they learned and share what they enjoy most about the fall season.

> *We've learned all about what people did in the fall long ago. They worked very hard to harvest food for the winter. Now, let's talk about the things people do in the fall today. What are some things you like to do in the fall? Gather leaves? Drink a cup of delicious apple cider? What are your favorite fall holidays? Great ideas, everyone. Autumn is an exciting season!*

Following Up

Invite children to explore the changes in fall foliage by doing leaf rubbings. If possible, take children on a nature walk to gather leaves of different colors and shapes. Alternatively, you can bring leaves into the classroom yourself. Provide children with crayons and paper and have them create impressions by placing the paper on top of the leaf and rubbing over it with a crayon. When children are finished, display the rubbings next to the real leaves and challenge children to guess which leaf made each rubbing.

Try This!

Point out to children that people are not the only ones who must prepare for the winter—animals work very hard in the autumn as well! Invite children to act out a fall forest scene by taking on the roles of various creatures. Chipmunks and squirrels can gather nuts, birds can build warm nests, rabbits can dig deep holes, and bears can get ready for a long winter of hibernation.

You can emphasize the historical aspect of this activity by asking children to imagine how they might have been dressed for a harvest long ago. The girls might be wearing long skirts or dresses and bonnets, and the boys might be wearing knickers and vests. How do these clothes affect children's movements? Do the clothes keep them warm as they work in the field?

BOOK Link

After digging up potatoes for their own fall harvest, children will enjoy reading ***The Enormous Potato*** by Aubrey Davis (Kids Can Press, 1998). In this retelling of a classic folktale, a potato grows so huge that the farmer must call on his wife, daughter, dog, and cat to help him dig it out of the ground. Ultimately, it is the tiny mouse who provides just enough extra muscle to harvest the potato—which is big enough to feed the entire town.

Catching
Snowflakes

This activity builds children's awareness of seasonal changes as they experience an imaginary winter snowstorm.

Overview

After discussing the changes in weather and environment that take place in winter, children take an imaginary walk outside to catch snowflakes, walk through deep snow, and build their own snowpeople. The activity concludes as children return to the circle to enjoy a favorite wintertime treat and share the experiences they had in the snow.

Getting Started

Begin by asking children what changes take place in the winter. (If you live in a warm climate, you can ask children to share what they may have learned about winter climates through books, television, or other media.) To spark children's ideas, ask questions such as the following.

What season comes after fall? That's right, winter. What kinds of clothes do people wear to stay warm in the winter? Sweaters, mittens, and scarves. What else happens in the winter? What is a special kind of winter weather? Yes, snow! What are some fun activities to do in the snow? Yes, you can ride on a sled. You can also build a snowman . . . or maybe a snowwoman! What else do you like to do in the winter?

When children have had a chance to share what they know about winter, tell them that together you are going to turn the classroom into a winter wonderland! Start by asking children to imagine that they are looking out a window. The sky is gray and it looks cold outside. Then suddenly, one little snowflake floats down past their eyes. Then another, and another! Now the world outside looks very white. It's time to get dressed to go outside!

Okay, everybody up. We're going to get ready to go out and play in all that beautiful snow! First, we must put on a snowsuit to help us keep dry. Put one leg in… now the other . . . pull that snowsuit up. Put in both arms. Now grab your zipper and pull. Zzzzip! Now it's time for scarves, hats, and mittens. Put a hat on your head. Wind a long scarf around your neck. Now put a mitten on each hand. We can't forget boots to keep our feet warm and dry. Put your feet in and pull those boots up. Now we are all ready to go outside for some wintertime fun!

Moving and Learning

Once children are suited up for the snow, it's time to go out the imaginary door and into the wonderland! Have children stand up in a circle and imagine that they are now outside. Give children images to encourage them to use their senses, such as: Can you feel the cold air on your face? Can you see the ground changing from brown to white as it gets covered with snow? Can you hear the wind blowing through the trees? Next, invite children to catch some snowflakes.

The snow is falling all around you. What do you think the snow tastes like? Try to catch some on your tongue to find out! Are a lot of snowflakes falling on your tongue at once, or are you catching one flake at a time? Can you catch the flakes on your finger first and look at them? What shapes do you see? How long does it take before the flakes melt?

After giving children time to enjoy catching their snowflakes, encourage them to imagine that the snow is much deeper now. Lead the group in walking around in a circle, asking children to lift their boots high for every step. It's hard work to trudge through the deep snow! Ask children to stop walking and stand in place as you divide the class into small groups. Direct each group to a different area and invite them to build snowpeople. Guide children through the process as follows.

Work with your group to scoop a lot of snow up from the ground. Pack it together to make a big ball of snow. Roll that snowball on the ground. It's getting bigger and bigger! Now it's time to make the next part of your snowpeople. Make another ball of snow. This one is a little smaller. Great! Now lift it up and place it on top of the first snowball. Whew, it's heavy! Work together! Next, make the head. This is the smallest snowball. Place it on top. Wow, look at all those snowpeople!

When children have had time to work on their snowpeople, invite them to give their snowman or snowwoman a special personality by adding imaginary costumes. They might create a clown snowman by adding a funny red nose and great big shoes, or an astronaut snowwoman in a special suit and helmet.

Wrapping Up

Call children back to the circle to share their experiences.

All right, everyone, let's come back inside from the snow. Why don't we all have a cup of hot cocoa to warm up? Pick up the cup and take a sip. Don't forget to blow on it first! It's very hot!

As children sip their imaginary cocoa, encourage them to talk about what it felt like to play in the snow. To get children talking, ask questions such as: Was it cold outside in the snow? Was it fun to work together? What kind of snowperson did you create with your group?

Following Up

Invite children to observe frost crystals firsthand with this simple science experiment. Gather several drinking glasses or glass jars and have children dip them quickly into a large tub of water (supervise closely for safety). Place the glasses immediately into a freezer, or outside on a very cold day. When the glasses become frosty, bring them back to the classroom and invite children to look closely at the glasses with a magnifier. They will see patterns that look just like snowflakes! Encourage children to draw the patterns on a sheet of paper. Then invite children to compare their drawings.

Try This!

There are a host of wintertime activities children can explore through movement. To extend winter fun, invite children to lie down on the floor and go "sledding" on their bellies. Children might also enjoy taking a turn on an imaginary ice-skating rink.

BOOK Link

Share ***The Jacket I Wear in the Snow*** by Shirley Nitzel (Greenwillow, 1989). Children will enjoy this cumulative story about the many articles of clothing a little girl must struggle into before going outside. The rebus illustrations add to the fun of this story—invite children to chime in with the correct word as you point to each picture.

A Sign of
Spring

This activity invites children to use their senses as they explore the changes and growth that take place in the spring.

Overview

Children experience the wonders of nature in the springtime by taking on the roles of animals and plants. Through movement, children become bears emerging from a long winter of hibernation, birds catching their first worm of the season, and seeds blooming into beautiful flowers. The activity concludes with an imaginary nature walk and an opportunity for children to share what they found on their excursion.

Getting Started

Gather children together to discuss what they know about the spring.

What season comes after winter? Yes, spring. What is the weather like in the spring? Does it begin to get warmer outside? How does the world around you change in the springtime? Do plants begin to grow? What is one of your favorite things to do in the spring?

Next, encourage children to think about what animals do in the springtime. Do they know what bears do? After hibernating all winter, bears come out of their caves and dens and into the warm sunlight. Invite children to share the experiences of the bears through movement as follows.

Imagine that you are a little bear in a dark and cozy den. Curl up in a little ball and close your eyes. Now you can feel the first warm breeze of spring blowing through your den. It's time to wake up! Open your eyes and take a nice stretch. Now get on your hands and knees and crawl out of your den. What do you see? Is the sun shining brightly? What do you smell? Are flowers growing? The little bears are thirsty! Let's find a stream. Make your way to the stream and take a sip of the sweet, cool water. After such a long winter, the bears are also very hungry! Look into the stream. Do you see fish swimming by? Okay, little bears, use your claws and catch yourself a delicious fish for breakfast. Yum!

Now I need all my bears to come back to the circle to find out what animal you will become next!

Moving and Learning

Tell children that the next animal they will become moves in a very special way—it flies! Ask children if they know what birds do in the spring. They catch worms and build nests. Invite children to stand up and begin spreading their wings for a springtime flight.

Okay, everyone, stand up and stretch your arms. Imagine that your arms are wings covered with feathers. It's time to fly! Flap your wings and fly around the room. Watch out for the other birds! Now look down to the ground. What do you see? It's a nice juicy worm! Fly down to the ground and pull that worm out of the soft ground with your beak. Terrific!

Now that it's spring, our birds might also need a new home—perhaps for starting a family. Gather twigs and grasses and build yourself a nest. You all look very cozy in your new homes!

Gather children back to the circle and point out that animals are not the only ones who are active in the spring—plants are very busy growing, too! Invite children to become tiny seeds for the next step of the activity.

Everyone find a spot on the floor and curl up into a little seed. Now I'm coming around and I'm digging a little hole for each of you—go ahead, roll right in! I'd really like my flowers to grow, so I'm going to give them some water. Here comes some nice warm sunshine, too! Now my little seeds are beginning to pop up through the dirt. A little more water, a little more sun . . . My flowers are really starting to grow now! Stretch up, up, up, flowers! Look at them bloom, how beautiful!

Great job, everyone! Before we come back to the circle, I'd like you to change from the flowers back into yourselves. Great! Now, imagine

Classroom Management

TIP

If a child is having trouble focusing, invite him or her to take a walk around the room with you. Point out imaginary sights and sounds, such as a beautiful flower or a bubbling brook.

you are taking a nice spring walk. Walk through the room. What do you see, hear, and smell? Find one special thing to bring back to the circle. It could be a flower or even a ladybug. Ready? Great! Everyone come back to the circle and we will share our springtime treasures.

Wrapping Up

Once children are seated back in the circle, invite them to share what they found on their nature walk. Encourage children to hold what they found in their hands and show it to the rest of the group by describing the object. Ask children questions such as: What color is your bug? Does it have wings? Can you point to the wings? Help children develop a visual image by encouraging them to use size, shape, and color words.

Following Up

Invite children to create a group poem about the spring. Explain to children that they can create a poem in free verse—this means it does not have to rhyme. Ask each child to name one thing they enjoy about the spring—a favorite animal, plant, or outdoor activity they do themselves. As each child shares his or her ideas, write one sentence on chart paper. When the poem is complete, have children create illustrations for the line they dictated. You might even invite children to read their poem into a tape recorder. Now you have sound, image, and written text!

Try This!

Invite children to explore the special sounds of spring by playing a nature tape or CD. Choose a recording that includes springtime sounds, such as a babbling brook, chirping birds, and so on. As children listen, invite them to close their eyes and imagine what they might see to go along with the sounds they hear. Can they see the water rushing? Are the birds hopping among the branches of a tree? Provide paper and crayons and invite children to draw what they saw in their mind's eye. Display the pictures on a bulletin board or bind them together to create a class book.

BOOK Link

After learning about what animals do in the springtime, children will enjoy reading *It's Spring!* by Samantha Berger and Pamela Chanko (Scholastic Hello Reader, 2000). The rhyming text follows a chain of animals as they inform one another of the springtime changes taking place. The seasonal game of telephone ends when at last the birds begin to sing—to tell the bears, "Wake up, it's spring!"

Beach
Adventure

This activity invites children to participate in summertime fun as they explore a sunny seashore environment.

Overview

After discussing the many things that make summer special, children are invited to take an imaginary trip to the beach. Children explore the environment by wading in the water, collecting seashells, building a sandcastle, and pairing off for a game of catch with a beach ball. The activity concludes as children return to the circle to share an item they found at the beach and talk about their experiences there.

Getting Started

Invite children to share what they know about the summer season by introducing the day's activity.

> Today we're going to explore a special season. It is the warmest season of the year. Most children do not have school during this season. Some of you may go on vacations with your family, or you may go to camp. Can anyone guess what season we're going to explore today? Yes, summer! What do you like to do in the summertime? Do you visit family? Play outdoors? Summer is also a great time to go to the beach. What are some things you like to do at the beach? Swim? Play in the sand? Collect shells? Today you will get to try all these activities—we are going to go on a beach adventure right here in the classroom!

Encourage children to get ready for their day at the beach by packing a pretend beach bag. Invite children to name supplies they might need, such as a bathing suit, pail and shovel, and a snack.

All right, everyone, are your beach bags packed? Great! Now, there's one last thing we must do before playing in the sun. Put on sunscreen! This is very important to protect your skin. Hold a bottle of sunscreen in one hand. Now squeeze the bottle and put some lotion in your other hand. Great! Now put that lotion all over your skin. Don't forget to cover each and every part. Terrific! Now we are ready to go!

Moving and Learning

Invite children to stand up and imagine that the classroom has turned into a warm, sunny beach. What do they see? Sand and water? What do they hear? The waves crashing against the shore? Encourage children to explore the environment by taking an imaginary walk on the sand.

Okay, everyone, follow me! We're going to take a walk down to the water's edge. How does the sand feel underneath your feet? Is it warm and soft? Can you feel it between your toes? Now try dipping your toe in the water. Brrr, it's cold! Let's wade in a little farther. The water is up to our waists now. Watch out for the waves! Now, let's walk along the shore and look for seashells. What kinds of seashells do you see? Are they large or small? What colors are they? Pick some up and put them into your beach bag.

Once children have had a chance to explore the environment, invite them to take out their pails and shovels and build a sand castle. Guide children's movements by asking them specific questions, for example: Are you digging deep in the sand with your shovel? Can you fill your pail all the way up with sand? What will your castle look like? How does the sand feel in your fingers?

When children have had time to build, invite them to choose a partner for another beach activity—a game of catch with a beach ball.

Everyone stand up and face your partner. Pick up a beach ball. Is it a big ball? Do you have to hold it in both hands? Go ahead, try a game of catch! Throw the ball to your partner. Since we're using an imaginary ball, it will help if you make eye contact with your partner.

Classroom Management

TIP

Depending on the needs of your classroom, you may wish to assign children partners for their game of catch, rather than having them choose their own. You might use the opportunity to pair up children who don't often play together, giving them a chance to interact within an organized framework.

If you look in your partner's eyes, you'll know when the ball is being thrown. Try a high throw! Try a low throw! Can you roll the ball to each other? Great!

We've had a wonderful time at the beach today. I'd like everyone to find one thing to bring back with you. It might be a beautiful shell, some sand, or even a handful of seaweed! Now, let's return to the circle and talk about our day at the beach.

Wrapping Up

Gather children back to the circle and give them a chance to discuss their beach adventure. Ask questions such as: What was your favorite activity to do at the beach? Which do you like better, playing in the sand or in the water? Invite children to share their imaginary beach souvenirs with the group. Encourage children to talk about the size, shape, color, and texture of the object.

Following Up

Build children's sorting and classifying skills by inviting them to explore real seashells. Children may have seashell collections from family vacations that they can bring into the classroom, or you can purchase seashells at most craft supply stores. Provide children with sorting trays or clean, empty egg cartons. Encourage them to compare the seashells and sort them by a variety of criteria, such as size, shape, and color.

Try This!

Another summertime activity children might enjoy is tree climbing. Invite children to stand up and imagine their own tree right in front of them. Encourage children to pantomime climbing movements, grabbing on to branches and moving up the tree. Ask children to describe how the world looks from up high. They might even find a surprise up in their tree, such as a nest of bird's eggs just ready to hatch!

BOOK Link

Invite children to share a dog's-eye view of a summer vacation by reading **Sally Goes to the Beach** by Stephen Huneck (Harry Abrams, 2000). Children will enjoy following the Labrador retriever's adventures in the sand and surf as they explore the beautiful woodcut print illustrations.

Imagination
Sensation

This activity helps build observation skills as children explore the five senses.

Overview

After identifying the five senses and the body parts they use to experience them, children use their imagination to explore taste, sight, smell, touch, and sound. Children will have the opportunity to imagine tasting their favorite foods, touching the soft down of a newborn chick, and listening to a variety of sounds. The activity concludes with a review of the five senses and a chance for children to share their favorite sights, smells, tastes, sounds, and textures.

Getting Started

Gather children in a circle and help them to identify the five senses by inviting them to chime in with the words that complete the following sentences.

There are five senses. Let's see if we can name them together. We use our eyes to . . . see. We use our ears to . . . hear. We use our nose to . . . smell. We use our fingers to . . . touch. We use our tongue to . . . taste. Great job!

We are going to use our imagination to explore all five of our senses. We're going to start with taste—I hope you're all hungry!

Moving and Learning

Remaining in the circle, guide children in exploring each of their senses with the following verbal cues. You may choose to explore all five senses in one day, or extend the exploration over several days. As you guide children through the activities, be sure to give them plenty of time to respond and share their ideas and experiences with the group.

Taste

What is one of your favorite foods? Corn on the cob with butter? Pancakes with syrup? A juicy orange? Choose one of your very favorites. Picture the food in front of you. Is it on a plate? Will you use a knife and fork to eat it, or pick it up in your hands? Now it's time to taste our foods. Lift the food to your mouth. Try to taste the flavors—is it sweet? Sour? Tangy? How does the food feel in your mouth? Soft? Crunchy? Eat it all up. Yum! How can you move to show you are enjoying your food? Rub those bellies, everyone! Now, imagine one of your least favorite foods. Take a bite! Is it bitter, salty, spicy? How about washing it down with your favorite drink? Go ahead and take a sip! Mmmm. That's better!

Sight

When we were eating our foods, we were using the sense of sight as well as taste. Do you remember how I asked you to picture your food? What color was it? What shape? How about the shape of your plate? What kind of glass or cup did you take your drink out of? Lean forward and look closely. Point to each object as you picture it. What are some other things you like to look at? A beautiful sunset? A fireworks display? Close your eyes and picture it. What colors and shapes do you see?

Smell

Another important sense we use while eating is smell. What does your favorite food smell like? How about your least favorite food? What are some of your other favorite smells? How about flowers? Picture some colorful flowers just in front of you. Are they in a vase or growing in the ground? Go ahead and pick them up. Hold them close to your

Classroom Management

TIP

Ask children who need extra encouragement to imagine sensations associated with different settings, for example, a favorite smell from home (cookies baking), a sound from school (the bell ringing), or something they might see at the playground (a jungle gym).

nose and smell them! Do they smell sweet? What about a smell that you don't like? Onions? A musty basement? What don't you like about that smell? How can you show that something doesn't smell good? Pinch your nose with your fingers!

Touch

Now we're going to explore our sense of touch. Imagine there is a tiny little chick in front of you with soft yellow down. Very gently, reach out with a finger and touch its soft fur. Now carefully pick up the chick and touch it to your cheek. How does it feel? Animal skins have very different textures. There's rough alligatorskin, dry snakeskin, smooth and wet sealskin. Reach out and touch any animal you like. Is it furry, sticky, smooth?

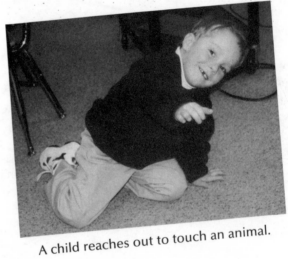

A child reaches out to touch an animal.

Sound

Next, we're going to explore hearing. I'm going to call out some ideas, and I want you to imagine each sound in your mind. Cup your ear with your hand. Nod your head to show me that you hear each sound. Ready? Listen carefully! Imagine . . .

*a doorbell ringing
a dog barking far away
a dog barking close by
a car horn honking
a rushing stream
a crowd cheering at a baseball game
a basketball bouncing on the pavement
your favorite music.
Terrific job, everyone!*

Wrapping Up

When children have had time to explore each sense, invite them to share their favorites with the group. What was their favorite thing to eat? What smells do they like best? What sounds are special to them? Conclude the activity by helping children summarize what they learned.

Today we explored all five of our senses. We learned that our bodies help us to see, hear, smell, touch, and taste.

Following Up

Invite children to create a class book celebrating each of the five senses. Provide children with drawing paper and crayons and ask them to draw a picture of something they like to taste, touch, see, smell, or hear. Help children create captions for their pictures. Then invite children to work in small groups to create a cover and divider pages with labels for each sense. Put the pages in order, bind them together, and add the book to your classroom library.

Try This!

Invite children to make observations with all of their senses by visiting a variety of imaginary places. You might take a trip to explore the sights and sounds of the jungle, the tastes and smells of a bakery, and so on. As you explore each environment, encourage children to name things they can see, hear, taste, smell, and touch. Then invite children to make their own suggestions of places they'd like to visit.

BOOK Link

For a humorous (yet scientifically accurate) look at the five senses, read *You Can't Taste a Pickle with Your Ear* by Harriet Ziefert (Handprint, 2002). Each sense gets its own section and is explored through vivid imagery and playful rhyming text.

From
Head to Toe

This activity reinforces basic science concepts as children identify the many parts that make up the human body.

Overview

After a warm-up in which they respond to directives through a series of movements, children are invited to name various body parts and explore what each can do. The activity concludes with a review of what children have learned and a discussion about ways to keep the body healthy.

Getting Started

Seat children in a circle and explain that they will be doing an activity to learn about the many things their bodies can do. Begin by asking children to name different ways they can make their bodies move.

What are some things you can do with your body? How can you make it move? Yes, you can walk. You can run. You can jump. You can make your body move quickly. You can make it move slowly.

Okay, everybody stand up. I'm going to call out one word at a time. You can respond in any way you like with your bodies. Ready? It's time to . . . jump, turn, hop, twist, kick, bend, curl, reach up, reach down, reach sideways, reach backward, reach forward

Great job, everyone! Now, your body may feel a little tired from all that movement. Let's take a seat. What is something we can do for our bodies to help them feel energetic again? Rest. Let's take a couple of nice, deep breaths. Next, we're going to learn about all the things we can do with our bodies' many parts.

Moving and Learning

Begin a discussion of how the body works by asking children how their bodies knew what to do as you called out your directions. Explain that one of the most important parts of their body is the brain. The brain is the part that thinks, and it sends messages to all the other parts to tell them what to do. Invite children to stand up in a circle and explore what each part of their bodies can do, as follows.

Okay, everyone, we're going to start from the top of our bodies and work our way down. What part is at the very top of your body? Your head!

Move your head around in a circle. Move it up and down. Now side to side. Great! Next, we have our arms. Reach one arm up. Reach high into the sky! Now do it with the other arm. Now both arms. Terrific!

Continue to work your way from head to toe, asking children to name each body part and inviting them to move it in different ways. Be sure to include hands, fingers, waists, tummies, legs, feet, and toes. When children have named and explored all of their many parts, invite them to wind down, as follows.

Let's finish by giving our whole bodies one last shake. Ready? Shake all those sillies out. Now take a nice deep breath. Very good. Let's sit down in our circle and talk about what we learned today!

Wrapping Up

Help children to review the body part names they learned by pointing to your head, neck, shoulders, and so on, asking children to point to the same part on their own bodies and call out its name. Conclude the activity with a discussion of ways children can keep their bodies healthy and strong.

What are some things we can do for our bodies to help keep them healthy? We can eat healthy foods, like fruits and vegetables. We can drink a lot of water. We can exercise. We can rest and get plenty of sleep. Doing these things will help keep our bodies working hard for us!

Following Up

Invite children to display their learning visually by doing body tracings. Divide the class into pairs and provide each pair with a large sheet of craft paper and markers. Have one partner lie down on the paper as the other partner traces the outline of his or her body. Then have children work together to label each part. Children might also enjoy adding on body parts with collage materials, such as yarn for hair, buttons for eyes, and so on.

Try This!

By digesting food, the body gets the energy it needs to keep running. Invite children to tell what they know about digestion. Explain that food travels down a tube into the stomach. Inside the stomach, body parts called intestines break food down so that the body can use food for energy. Invite one child to act as the "food" while other children play different body parts. For instance, two children can form a circle with their arms to create a "mouth" for the food to go through, and children can line up in two rows to create a path for the food!

BOOK Link

For further anatomy adventures, read **Me and My Amazing Body** by Joan Sweeney (Crown, 1999). The lively text and simple illustrations allow children to explore the human body, inside and out, on a level they can understand.

Classroom Management

TIP

To avoid accidents during movement activities, have children stand several feet apart from one another. Ask them to test their movement space by stretching out their arms and turning in a circle. If they can do this without touching another child, they are ready to start moving!

Catch the
Feeling

This activity reinforces descriptive vocabulary as children explore a range of emotions through body language and movement.

Overview

Children identify different types of feelings by sharing experiences they have had in their own lives (times when they felt happy, sad, and so on). They are then invited to react to a series of imaginary objects through movement, as they express various emotions through body language. Next, children act out a journey to an imaginary place in which feelings are the focus. The activity concludes with an opportunity for children to share their experiences and the vocabulary they learned.

Getting Started

Begin a discussion about feelings by asking children to tell about a time when they felt happy. To get children started, offer a few suggestions such as: Are you happy when you get a new toy? Are you happy when you play with your pet? Continue asking children to share experiences they have had with different emotions, such as times when they felt excited, scared, or angry. Next, introduce the concept of body language by asking children to identify the feelings associated with different facial expressions and movements.

If you saw Miranda frowning and stamping her feet, how would you think she was feeling? That's right, angry. If Vincent were smiling and jumping up and down, what might he be feeling? Yes, he might be very happy. He also might be excited.

After introducing several feelings to the group, invite children to stand up and use their own bodies to show different feelings. As children stand in a circle, encourage them to imagine that there is a special box right in front of them. The box is magical—each time it is opened, there is a new item inside! Guide children to use body language to show their feelings as they react to each object.

I'm going to open up our magic box. Let's see what's inside. The box is full of candy and treats! How does that make you feel? Are you happy? How can you use your body to show you are happy? Yes, you can smile. Try jumping up and down. Try clapping your hands. Great! Now I'm going to close the box. What do you think we'll see next? Let's open the box again. Oh, my! A very big monster is inside! That monster is making us feel scared. How can you show you are scared? You might hide your face with your hands. You might start to run away! Let's all run in place. Good job, everyone!

Continue to open and close the box, discovering a different object each time and guiding children to express different feelings through verbal cues. You can also ask children to suggest their own ideas for objects, and show how these things make them feel.

Moving and Learning

Tell children that they are going to take an imaginary trip to a special place. Many things will happen to them in that place, and they will have a chance to act out their feelings about each one. Suggest an environment (for example, the beach) and invite children to stand up and imagine being in that place.

Is everyone ready for a day at the beach? It is warm and sunny and there is sand between your toes. The waves are crashing on the sand. Now, let's see what kinds of feelings we will have on the beach. Here we go! What might happen that makes us feel sad on the beach? A crab just bit us on the toe! Yeooowww! Grab your toe and hop up and down. How can you show you are sad? You might frown. You might cry a little bit. Okay, now something is going to happen to make us feel better. What is something that might make us feel surprised? Finding a buried treasure chest! What a surprise! Go ahead and start digging. As you are digging up the box your feelings might be changing. You are getting excited to see what's inside! Now, what might happen that makes us feel disappointed? The treasure box is locked! How can you show you are disappointed? Now, how can we end our trip with something happy? You found the key! Open up the box. Look at all that treasure!

Classroom Management

TIP

You may find that there are some children who express difficult emotional experiences in their discussion and creative play. Offer support by encouraging students to express their feelings in appropriate ways. You can also assure children that everyone has both happy and sad times in their lives.

As you narrate events, give children suggestions for ways to express their feelings through movement. You can also invite children to suggest their own events and feelings. Repeat the activity as many times as you like, using a different environment each time.

Wrapping Up

Gather children together and encourage them to talk about the different feelings they had on their trip. Help children to review the vocabulary they learned by asking them to name the feelings associated with different movements and expressions, for example, How might you feel if you are frowning? Sad.

How might you feel if you are smiling and laughing? Happy. Continue the discussion by asking children to tell how they used their faces and bodies to express each feeling.

Following Up

Invite children to play a game of "feelings charades." Write several different words for feelings on small pieces of paper and place them in a bag. Invite one child up in front of the group and have the child choose a word from the bag. Then ask the child to act out the word without naming it as the group calls out their guesses. The child who guesses the feeling picks the next word. Continue until all children have had a chance to act out at least one word.

Try This!

You can use the "imaginary journey" format to reinforce many different kinds of vocabulary and grammatical concepts. For example, to teach prepositional phrases, children might take a trip over the rainbow or under the sea. Or you might reinforce verbs by having children act out action words during their trip: they can walk to the playground, ride on the seesaw, and slide down the slide.

To help children find the correct vocabulary word for an emotion, ask specific questions related to their own experiences, such as: How do you feel when you've done your best work? or How do you feel when a friend has a toy you really want to play with? You can also help to extend children's vocabulary by suggesting new words. For example, when children discover that the treasure box is locked, they might feel frustrated instead of simply feeling angry.

BOOK Link

For a story that incorporates many different emotions, read *I Feel Happy and Sad and Angry and Glad* by Mary Murphy (Dorling Kindersley, 2000). Children will identify with the feelings expressed by Milo and Ellie as they have fun together, disagree, and make up again during their play. The simple first-person narrative and sweet illustrations demonstrate to children that it's all right to have strong feelings, and help them to find the right words to express them.

Becoming a Butterfly

This activity builds children's awareness of growth and change as they explore life cycles.

Overview

After discussing the changes that various animals go through as they grow, children explore a butterfly's life cycle through movement. By following verbal cues, children become crawling caterpillars, form a chrysalis, and emerge as beautiful butterflies. The activity culminates in a discussion of children's own dreams for when they themselves reach adulthood.

Getting Started

Gather children in a circle and begin a discussion about the physical changes different creatures go through as they reach adulthood.

> *Today we are going to learn about life cycles. All creatures grow and change as they get older. What are people born as? Babies. How do ducks begin their lives? As ducklings! And cows are born as . . . calves. What about frogs? Yes, frogs are born as tadpoles. Do they look like frogs? How are they different? They have a long tail and no legs. Do they grow up to look like their parents? Yes, they do! Some creatures look the same way when they are born as they will look when they grow older. Some look very different.*

Tell children that they will be exploring the life cycle of a creature that goes through many changes as it grows—a butterfly. Butterflies start life as caterpillars. Next, they form a hard shell around themselves called a chrysalis. Inside the chrysalis, they grow and change until they come out as . . . butterflies!

Moving and Learning

Now it is time for children to get moving! Invite them to see for themselves what it feels like to become a butterfly by following your verbal directions.

> *All right everyone, we are all going to start out as caterpillars. Imagine that you have many, many legs but no arms! Are you fuzzy? How do you move around? Okay, get on your hands and knees and start crawling! Find yourself a stem to climb. Can you crawl out onto a leaf? Caterpillars eat a lot of leaves, so take a bite! How does it taste? Now look around you. What does the world look like to a caterpillar? The stalks of grass? The sneakers of a child running by? A drop of rain falling beside you? You are very small, so all these things must look very big to you!*

When children have had time to explore life as a caterpillar, it is time to form a chrysalis. Encourage each child to find a spot in the room to create their new homes. Children can approximate this process by turning around in a small, tight circle. Next, invite children to imagine what it is like to be inside the chrysalis.

> *Now you are inside your chrysalis. Is it dark? Quiet? Does it feel safe? Now very, very slowly, your body is beginning to change. You begin to grow wings. Stretch out those arms! Try flapping your wings. It's difficult, because you are wrapped up so tightly. So, now it is time to come out! You are coming out of your chrysalis slowly. Now stretch those wings . . . and fly! All of the caterpillars have turned into beautiful butterflies.*

Invite children to flap their wings and "fly" around the room as butterflies. Then ask children to fly back to the circle to share their experiences.

A plant and a chrysalis.

Wrapping Up

Invite children to share what it felt like to start out as a caterpillar and grow into a butterfly. What were some of the changes that took place? How are caterpillars and butterflies different? Then ask children to think about their own life cycles.

> *How were you different as a baby from the way you are now? Do you look different? Move differently? What can you do now that you could not do as a baby? How do you think you will change as you grow older?*

Invite children to share any dreams they may have for their own future, such as traveling to distant lands, starting families of their own, and so on. Conclude the activity by helping children summarize what they learned.

> *Today we discovered that all creatures have life cycles. They change and grow as they get older. And as you get older, you will continue to change and grow too!*

Following Up

To give children firsthand experience in watching butterflies grow, you might consider ordering larvae for your classroom. Be sure to check your calendar before you order—you'll want to be sure that the weather will be warm at the time you will be releasing the butterflies, and that children will be in school. As they observe the larvae, encourage children to keep science journals. They can draw pictures to track the changes that take place. When the butterflies are ready, you can have a releasing ceremony outdoors and watch them fly free! Many companies provide this service to classrooms. One you might try is Insect Lore Products, P.O. Box 1535, Shafter, CA 93263; (800) LIVE-BUG (http://www.insectlore.com/).

Try This!

Children can explore the life cycle of almost any animal through movement. Using the same format, invite children to grow from puppies to dogs, kittens to cats, or tadpoles to frogs. Encourage children to pay special attention to how these animals move differently as they grow. Children might especially enjoy crawling as babies and then learning to walk as they grow into themselves!

As children become butterflies, remind them that the world looks very different from when they were caterpillars. Now they can see everything from above as they fly through the sky. Calling attention to this change in perspective will enrich children's experiences and help them to recognize important life–cycle changes.

BOOK Link

Read ***Waiting for Wings*** by Lois Ehlert (Harcourt, 2001). The rhyming text and beautiful cut-paper illustrations celebrate the butterfly's metamorphosis in this innovative picture book. The pages become increasingly larger as the story progresses, mirroring the growth and change that takes place during the life cycle.

On the Farm

This activity enriches children's science and social studies learning as they explore the work that goes into running a farm.

Overview

After identifying various jobs on a farm and discussing their importance, children work with partners to act out doing these jobs themselves. As they proceed through their day's work, children explore responsibility, caretaking, and working together toward a common goal. The activity concludes as children share an imaginary object brought back from the farm and discuss their experiences.

Getting Started

Gather children together and ask if any of them have ever seen or visited a farm. What kinds of animals can be found on a farm? There are sheep, cows, horses, goats, chickens, and pigs. And who takes care of the animals? The farmers. Encourage children to name the various jobs a farmer does.

> *How do farmers take care of their animals? Yes, all the animals need to be fed and watered. What about the chickens' eggs? Every day the eggs need to be gathered. What about the cows? What food do cows provide to people? That's right, milk. The cows need to be milked each day. What do we use sheep's wool for? Sheep's wool is used to make people's clothes. The sheep need to be sheared—this is like giving them a haircut!*

Explain to children that many farms also grow foods such as corn, wheat, fruit, and vegetables. This involves a lot of hard work as well! Farmers must plant seeds for the food, water the plants, and pick them when they are ready. Tell children that they are going to take on jobs and act out taking care of their own farm.

Moving and Learning

Divide the class into partners and assign each pair a different job. Once the jobs have been chosen, it's time to start the day's work!

Everyone join your partner and go to the area of the farm you will be working in. When you hear the rooster crow, it's time to start your jobs! Ready? Cock-a-doodle-doo! Remember to work with your partner. We can get a lot done if we all work together!

When children have had plenty of time to explore their jobs, ask them to finish up their work and return to the circle. Encourage partners to bring something back from their section of the farm to share with the group, such as a bucket of milk, a vegetable or fruit, or a fresh egg.

Mucking out the stalls.
Riding the horses.

Wrapping Up

Invite children to share their imaginary farm objects with the group and talk about the jobs they did. When children have had a chance to discuss their experiences, help them to articulate the ways in which farms help people.

Following Up

Once children have experienced working on a farm, they might enjoy building a miniature farm in the block center. Divide the class into small groups and have each group work on a different section of the farm. Children can build silos, barns, chicken coops, and a corral. They might even plant "a block orchard!"

Try This!

To reinforce children's understanding of the importance of doing jobs and working together, invite them to act out the work they do in another environment—their own homes. Ask children what kinds of responsibilities they have at home, such as taking care of a pet, setting the table, or cleaning up their toys. Using the same structure, assign pairs of children to different areas of the "house" to do their jobs.

BOOK Link

For a humorous take on life on the farm, read ***Giggle, Giggle, Quack*** by Doreen Cronin (Simon & Schuster, 2002). When Farmer Brown goes off on a vacation, he asks his brother Bob to take care of the farm and leaves him written instructions. What Bob doesn't know is that Duck knows how to use a pencil, and has replaced these instructions with his own.

Note

As partners choose their jobs, assign each pair to a different area of the room to work in. As children do their jobs, encourage them to look at different areas of the farm to see all the work that is going on! Children's farming jobs can include:

◆ caring for chickens, collecting eggs

◆ feeding and milking cows

◆ planting and watering seeds

◆ harvesting fruits and vegetables

◆ shearing sheep

◆ grooming and walking horses

◆ repairing barns and stalls

Dino

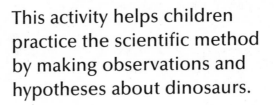

Dig

This activity helps children practice the scientific method by making observations and hypotheses about dinosaurs.

Overview

Through discussion, children learn the attributes of different species of dinosaurs. They are then invited to become scientists and dig up their own dinosaur fossils. After discussing the differences between herbivores, carnivores, and omnivores, children use movement to become herbivorous dinosaurs searching for plants to eat. The activity concludes with a discussion of children's experiences and an opportunity to make hypotheses based on observations about their own play.

Getting Started

Gather children together and invite them to share what they know about dinosaurs. Familiarize children with basic facts about dinosaurs and specific features of a few species.

Are dinosaurs alive today? No. Dinosaurs lived long, long ago. There were many different types of dinosaurs. Do you have a favorite? If you could be a dinosaur, which kind would you be? A Brachiosaurus with a long, long neck? Or a Triceratops with three horns? Maybe you'd be the biggest dinosaur of them all, the Tyrannosaurus rex!

Next, ask children how they think people know what different dinosaurs looked like. Scientists have found ancient dinosaur bones and fossils in the ground. Fossils are the remains of animals or plants that lived millions of years ago.

When scientists examine fossils, they can picture what the dinosaur looked like. Invite children to become scientists and dig up their own dinosaur fossils.

> *Okay, everybody stand up and grab a shovel. Many dinosaurs were huge, so let's spread out. Scientists dig up fossils very, very carefully. Now, let's all dig down into the dirt. Does anyone see anything yet? Yes? Okay, let's take out our brushes and wipe away the dust and the dirt. Hmmm . . . can you see the shape of the dinosaur's head? Is there a tail? Wow! We found a whole dinosaur!*

Suggest that children "send" the fossil they found to a museum. Then it's time to get ready to move, as children will become dinosaurs themselves!

Moving and Learning

Tell children that they will be learning more about dinosaurs by acting out their movements. Begin this part of the activity by asking children what it might have been like to be a dinosaur.

> *How did dinosaurs move? Some moved very slowly because they were so big. They had a lot of weight to carry around! What did dinosaurs eat? Some dinosaurs ate meat. Those dinosaurs are called* carnivores. *Some dinosaurs ate plants. Those are called* herbivores. *The dinosaurs that ate both plants and meat are called* omnivores. *Today we are going to try becoming herbivores. This means we will be looking for delicious plants to eat!*

Invite children to stand up as they become plant-eating dinosaurs. Encourage them to imagine that the classroom has become a valley full of bushes, grasses, trees, and water. Guide them through the activity with verbal cues, as follows:

> *Everybody up! It's time to become dinosaurs. You're growing, growing, growing . . . now you are a dinosaur. How big are you? How do you move? Is it hard to lift up those big, heavy legs? Dinosaurs needed to eat a lot of food. Since we're herbivores, let's look for some plants. Walk around the valley. What plants do you see? It looks like the most delicious leaves are all the way up in the tops of the trees! Stretch your neck up, up, up. Can you reach that leaf? Great! Grab it with your teeth and take a bite.*

> *Okay, everyone, it's time for the dinosaurs to take a rest. On the count of three, I want you to change back into yourselves. Ready? 1 . . . 2 . . . 3. Good job! Now, let's come back to the circle and talk about what it was like to be a dinosaur!*

Classroom Management

TIP

As children act out the movements of dinosaurs, circulate throughout the room and offer encouragement. To keep children focused, guide them with questions such as: What would a dinosaur look like walking through a muddy swamp? How would it move its enormous legs? If a child is having difficulty getting started, you might work with him or her to lumber, crawl, stomp, and so on.

Wrapping Up

Give children a chance to share what they enjoyed about becoming dinosaurs. Then help children focus on the plant-eating portion of the activity and invite them to make observations.

When you were looking for leaves to eat, was it hard to reach the leaves on the tops of the trees? What did you have to do? You had to stretch your necks all the way up. Now, can you guess why many herbivores had very long necks? That's right, so they could reach the leaves high in the treetops!

Explain to children that they have just done what scientists do—they have made hypotheses, or guesses, based on what they observed. Since there are no dinosaurs alive today, scientists have a difficult job. They must make hypotheses based on what they discover.

Following Up

Invite children to sharpen their powers of observation by creating their own fossils. Explain that some fossils are impressions of objects left in rocks. Provide children with play dough and various small objects such as twigs, leaves, or even toy animals. Have children flatten a piece of dough with the palm of their hand and press an object into the dough to create an impression. Display the "fossils" on one side of a table. Place the real objects on the other side of the table, and challenge children to guess which object made each fossil.

Try This!

Invite children to research different species of dinosaurs. Help them to find information in the library or on the Internet. Encourage children to find out what each dinosaur looked like, how it moved, and what it ate. You can do a different movement activity for each species children learn about. You might even have a dinosaur parade and invite each child to role-play a different dinosaur.

Note

Work with children to help them decide what kind of dinosaur they have discovered. They can use the facts they learned in their previous discussion. For instance, if the dinosaur has a long neck it might be a Brachiosaurus. If it has three horns, it might be a Triceratops. By using prior knowledge along with observation, children begin to learn how to use the scientific method to make discoveries.

BOOK Link

For a fanciful look at prehistoric creatures, read ***A Boy Wants a Dinosaur*** by Hiawyn Oram (Farrar Straus Giroux, 1990). Children will enjoy following the adventures of Alex, a boy who brings home a pet dinosaur named Fred. Not surprisingly, the enormous Fred wreaks havoc both at home and at school. When Alex wakes up and realizes it was all a dream, he decides he really does want a pet—a small, cuddly rabbit that will not be named Fred!

Animal
Adventures

This activity helps children learn about the needs of different animals as they care for an imaginary pet.

Overview

After sharing prior knowledge about animals and pets, children are invited to "adopt" an imaginary baby animal of their own. As children feed, nurture, and play with their pets, they learn about responsibility as well as the habits of different animals. The activity concludes as children introduce their pet to the group and share the ways in which they took care of it.

Getting Started

Draw on children's personal experiences with caring for animals by starting a discussion about pets.

Have you ever had a pet? What kinds of things do you have to do to care for a pet? What are some things that animals need? That's right, food and water. They also need to exercise and have fun.

Tell children that today they will be caring for an imaginary baby animal in the classroom. Help children choose their animals by making a few suggestions. Explain that since their pet will be imaginary, it can be any animal they choose. They might choose a realistic pet such as a puppy or kitten, or an exotic pet such as a baby whale, kangaroo, monkey, or even a lion cub. Once children have chosen their pets, assign each child an area of the classroom to work in. When children are settled in the spots you assigned, the animal adventures can begin!

Classroom Management

TIP

You might assign working areas for this activity by grouping together children who have chosen animals that live in similar habitats. For example, the block corner might become a jungle in which children care for baby monkeys and tiger cubs. The art center might represent a farm where children can take care of calves and piglets.

Moving and Learning

Tell children to imagine that their baby animal is in front of them. What does it look like? Does it have four legs and a tail? Does it have wings and feathers? Have children reach out and touch their imaginary pet. What does it feel like? Next, guide children in caring for their pets with verbal cues.

Your baby animal needs food and water. What does your animal eat? Fish? Lettuce? Hay? Meat? Please feed and water your pet so that it can grow big and strong. Good! Now that your baby has eaten, it needs to exercise and play. Go ahead and play alongside your animal. Try to move in the same way your pet does!

Now, after eating, exercising, and playing, it's time for the animals to take a rest. Cuddle up with your baby animal. Try to get your baby to sleep.

When children have had a chance to rest and wind down, invite them to bring their baby animal back to the circle to talk about their adventures.

Two children cuddle baby animals.

Wrapping Up

Encourage each child to introduce his or her pet to the class, tell what it looks like, where it lives, what it eats, and so on. Then invite children to share their experiences in caring for their pets. Was it hard work to take care of a baby animal? Which parts did they enjoy most?

Following Up

Invite children to create a lift-the-flap bulletin board about animal habitats. Provide each child with two sheets of paper, stapled together across the top. On the bottom sheet, have children draw the baby animal they took care of. On the top sheet, have them draw the place in which that animal lives. Attach children's work to a bulletin board. Encourage children to describe each habitat and guess which animal might live there. Then invite them to lift the flap and find out!

Try This!

In caring for pets, children take on parental roles. You can extend this idea by inviting children to role-play adult animals teaching their baby animals a skill they need to survive on their own. For instance, a mother bird might teach her baby bird how to fly, or a father bear might teach his cub how to catch a fish.

BOOK Link Invite children to have fun as they review the names of baby animals and their mothers by reading **Is Your Mama a Llama?** by Deborah Guarino (Scholastic, 1989.) The rhyming text follows Lloyd the llama as he asks a series of animals the same question: Is your mama a llama?

Pumpkin
Patch

This activity teaches children how plants grow as they enact the journey from seed to pumpkin.

Overview

After discussing what plants need to grow (soil, water, sunlight), children are invited to act out the growth cycle through movement. Starting out as a row of seeds, children move their bodies to gradually become a pumpkin vine in full bloom. After the pumpkins are "picked," children return to the circle to discuss what they learned about the stages of a pumpkin's growth.

Getting Started

Invite children to share what they know about plants and how they grow. Help children get started by connecting to their personal experiences.

Have you ever tried to grow a plant? What is something you need to grow plants? That's right, seeds. Where do you put the seeds? Yes, in soil, or in the ground. Soil has important vitamins plants need to grow. The soil acts like food for the plant. What else do plants need to grow? Yes, they need water. They also need sunlight.

Tell children that today they will be exploring how pumpkins grow. Explain that pumpkins grow on vines, and go through many stages before they are ready to be picked.

Moving and Learning

Have children stand in a row, close enough to one another to be able to grab hands. Tell them that the row will become a pumpkin vine, and that you will be the farmer who helps it grow. Begin the movement activity by having children curl up on the floor to become pumpkin seeds. Guide them through the stages of the pumpkins' growth with verbal cues, as follows.

Okay, everyone, curl your bodies up tight. Now I have a nice row of pumpkin seeds to plant. The first thing my seeds need is soil. I'm going to move down the row and dig a hole for each seed. The holes are ready. Roll in! Remember to stay in your row, pumpkin seeds.

Next, I need to cover the seeds with more soil. I'm going to pat some soil on top of each seed. Great! Now what else do my seeds need to grow? Water. I'm going to come down the row again, and spray each seed with a little water.

Now it's time for the pumpkins to start growing! First, my seeds will bloom into flowers. Make your body get a little bit bigger as you sprout out of the ground. Imagine that you are a beautiful pumpkin flower. Now the vine is beginning to form. Reach out your arms and grab the hands of the children next to you. Look at that beautiful pumpkin vine! Next, the pumpkins need sunlight. Imagine that the sun is shining down on the vine. Now the flowers are turning into tiny pumpkins. But the pumpkins aren't orange yet—they are green.

Keep holding hands as you grow bigger. Now, a little more water, a little more sunlight—my pumpkins are getting bigger and bigger! Slowly, uncurl your bodies as you grow on the vine. You're getting bigger, bigger, bigger . . . the pumpkins are finally ripe!

I'm going to come down the row and pick each big orange pumpkin off the vine. Now, let's return to the circle and talk about how our pumpkins grew.

Classroom Management

TIP

Use unhurried musical rhythms to set the tone for this activity. Create a slow, simple beat with an instrument such as a drum or maraca. As a class, discuss how the life cycle of a pumpkin plant takes time, usually from the very beginning of spring until the end of summer. Tell students to let the music guide their movements as they grow from seed to pumpkin.

Wrapping Up

Invite children to share their experiences as pumpkins growing on the vine. Which did they enjoy most, being a seed, a flower, or a full-grown pumpkin? Help children to review and summarize what they learned about the growth cycle by asking specific questions.

We learned that pumpkins start out as seeds. What do the seeds need to grow? What grows first on the vine? What color are the pumpkins before they turn orange?

Following Up

Enhance children's understanding of plant growth by allowing them to make their own discoveries with a classroom garden. Fill a window box with soil and invite children to make suggestions of objects to plant in the soil. Children might suggest realistic planting items such as apple or orange seeds, or more fanciful items such as a penny or a small toy. Accept all suggestions and plant the items in the soil, marking each planting spot with a label (you can make "flags" using toothpicks and small sticky notes). Place the planter in a sunny spot and water it daily. Encourage children to watch their garden and track which items sprout and which do not.

Try This!

Talk with children about the different ways people use pumpkins. They can be made into pumpkin pies, and of course, carved into jack-o'-lanterns. Jack-o'-lanterns can have all kinds of faces—they can be scary, funny, or friendly. For a fun extension, invite each child to think of a special personality for a jack-o'-lantern and act it out. Children might become pumpkin ballerinas, pumpkin kitties, or even pumpkin superheroes! Have children form a pumpkin vine by holding hands. As you "pick" each pumpkin off the vine, invite children to put on a short performance as their special pumpkin.

Enrich children's understanding of the growth cycle by using real props for this activity. Try using a play shovel to "dig" holes for the seeds. Fill a plant mister with water and give each child a small spray as you move down the row. You can also use a flashlight to act as the sun, shining it briefly on each child. Ask children to respond to the water and light by making their bodies into bigger shapes as the pumpkins grow.

BOOK Link

Read ***The Biggest Pumpkin Ever*** by Steven Kroll (Holiday House, 1984), a story about two mice who choose the same pumpkin to enter into the town's pumpkin-growing contest. Without being aware of the other's participation, one mouse takes care of the pumpkin during the day while the other cares for it at night. Children will delight in the whimsical illustrations as the mice unwittingly create the biggest pumpkin ever!

Waddle &

Nod

This activity introduces the concept of animal adaptation as children explore the habits and habitats of penguins.

Overview

After discussing what penguins look like and where they live, children learn how penguins adapt to their environment by imitating penguin movements. Through role-play, children explore how penguins waddle, slide, dive, swim, catch fish, carry eggs, and sleep standing up. The activity concludes as children review what they learned about penguins and the environments in which they live.

Getting Started

Begin by asking children to tell what they already know about penguins. What do they look like? What colors are they? If possible, show children pictures of penguins and ask them to describe what they see. Point out that penguins have short, torpedo-shaped bodies with small wings at their sides. But they don't use their wings to fly—they use them to swim! Invite children to stand up and move as they learn more about penguins.

Okay, everybody up. We are all going to become penguins! Put your arms close to your sides. These are your penguin wings. But remember, penguins can't fly, so keep your wings at your sides. Now, let's try walking. Penguins have very short legs and can hardly lift them, so you can take only very small steps. Now, you are waddling like a penguin!

Moving and Learning

Remind children that although penguins can't fly, they are birds. And how do birds have babies? They lay eggs! Explain that one type of penguin, called an emperor, takes care of its eggs in a very unusual way. It does not keep its eggs in a nest like other birds. It carries them on its feet! Invite children to become emperor penguins and practice carrying their eggs.

Imagine that there is a very delicate egg resting on your feet. You must be very careful with your egg—be sure not to break it! Now, let's try to inch forward. Take very small steps. Don't let that egg drop.

Tell children that after such a busy day, the penguins need to sleep. But penguins don't sleep the way people do. They sleep standing up! Encourage children to stand still, arms at their sides, and close their eyes. Then have them return to the circle to discuss what they learned.

Wrapping Up

Invite children to talk about all the things they did as penguins—waddle, slide, carry eggs, dive, swim, and take a nap. Which activity did they enjoy most? Help children to review what they learned by asking specific questions such as the following.

How are penguins different from most other birds? How does an emperor penguin take care of its eggs?

Following Up

Invite children to put on a penguin play. On chart paper, list facts children have learned about penguins: how they move, how they play, what they eat, how they sleep, and so on. Then have children stand in a line. As children take turns presenting each fact, the rest of the group can act it out through movement. You might invite family members or another class to see the performance.

Try This!

For further exploration of emperor penguins, try this penguin egg-pass game. Remind children that emperor penguins carry their eggs on their feet. Explain that after the mother penguin lays the egg, she goes out to sea to get food while the father penguin keeps it warm. The mother penguin stands very close to the father and passes him the egg—and they do this using only their feet! Have children take off their shoes and stand close together in a line. Place a round object, such as a tennis ball, on the feet of the first child. Then have him or her pass the "egg" to the next child in the line. Remind children that they can use only their feet to pass the egg. How many children can pass it before it drops? Encourage children to repeat the activity and keep a tally sheet to track their progress.

BOOK Link

For a story about emperor penguins, read ***The Little Penguin*** by A. J. Wood (Dutton, 2002). This charming, simply told story follows a newly hatched penguin as he loses his fuzzy gray down and matures into adulthood. Children will identify with the little penguin's desire to grow up as they follow his journey through the icy Antarctic—and they will also learn more about this special animal along the way.

Classroom Management

TIP

As children pretend to dive and swim, remind them to follow safety rules. They can approximate a diving movement with a small jump, and "swim" by walking slowly and moving their arms through the air. Remind them to watch closely for other children as they move.

Sun, Moon, & Stars

This activity introduces important science concepts as children explore what they see in the sky during day and night.

Overview

After discussing the differences between day and night, children learn about the sun, moon, and stars through movement. First, they explore the movement of the planets as they circle around the sun. Children then discover the stages of the moon as they create shapes with their bodies. Finally, children explore constellations as they role-play stars forming the Big Dipper. The activity concludes as children return to the circle to share what they learned.

Getting Started

Begin a discussion about day and night by tapping into children's prior knowledge. Guide them to explore the differences between the daytime and nighttime sky with questions such as the following.

How do you know when it is daytime? When you wake up in the morning, what do you see in the sky? During the day, is it dark or light outside? How do you know when it is nighttime? What can you see in the sky at night? Is the sky light or dark at night?

Tell children that they will be learning about the sun, moon, and stars by acting out their movements and positions in the sky.

Classroom Management

TIP

Be sure to repeat each portion of the activity several times, giving each child a chance to play the roles of sun, Earth, and stars. To give children plenty of time to explore their roles, you may wish to do each portion of the activity on a separate day.

Moving and Learning

Explain that the sun is actually a big, bright star that gives us light during the day. Invite children to explore how we get light from the sun by having them stand in a circle. Explain that they will be acting as the planets. There are many planets, and the one we live on is called Earth. Choose one child to play Earth, and one child to play the sun by standing in the middle of the circle. Provide the child playing the sun with a flashlight, and have that child shine the light. Then guide children to act out the movement of the planets around the sun, as follows.

All right, everyone, our sun is shining bright! Now, the sun stays in one place as the planets move around it in a circle. Planets, let's stay in our circle and move slowly around the sun.

Continue moving in a circle. Let children take turns playing the planets and the sun. When a few children have had an opportunity to play the sun, tell the class it is time to explore the nighttime sky.

What do we see in the sky at night? The moon. The moon looks different to us at different times. Let's all make our bodies into a big round circle. This is what the moon looks like when it is full. Then there are times that we can see only half of the moon. Let's work with partners to make this shape. I want one partner to stand up tall and straight. Now, partner number two, I want you to curve your body from your partner's head to their toes. Bend your arms and legs. Great half moons! Now, sometimes we see even less of the moon. Just a curved sliver. This is called a crescent moon. Everybody try it—curve your body to make a crescent. Beautiful!

A shining star.

What else do we see in the sky at night? That's right, stars. Have you ever noticed any patterns in the stars? The stars make patterns called constellations. One constellation is called the Big Dipper because it looks like a giant soup ladle! Now each of you will get a chance to be a star in the Big Dipper.

Help children form the shape of the Big Dipper by guiding them to stand in appropriate spots on the floor. Have a few children form the constellation. The rest of the group can pretend to gaze at the stars through telescopes, and describe what they see. Then have children switch roles.

Wrapping Up

Have children return to the circle to share their experiences. Which role did they enjoy playing most? Help children review what they learned about the differences in the sky during day and night.

During the day, we can see a star. We call that star the sun. Planets, including our Earth, circle the sun. They go around and around it.

Though the moon appears to have different shapes at different times, it's always the same shape. What shape is it? That's right! The moon is round like an orange.

Stars sometimes make up patterns or constellations in the sky. One constellation that's easy to spot is the Big Dipper. It's shaped just liked a soup ladle. A few minutes ago, each of us took a turn pretending to be a shining star in the Big Dipper.

Following Up

Invite children to learn more about the sun, moon, and stars by guiding them through a research project. List children's questions and topics of interest on chart paper. Then help them find the answers in library books or on the Internet. You can culminate the project by creating a class book. Have each child create a page illustrating one fact they learned, and have them dictate a sentence to go with the picture. Bind the pages together and add the book to your classroom library.

Try This!

There are several interesting Native American legends about how the sun, moon, and stars came to be in the sky. You can add a cultural dimension to your exploration by telling these legends and inviting children to take on different roles as they act out the story. Look for legends in folktale anthologies such as ***The Storytelling Star: Tales of the Sun, Moon, and Stars*** by James Riordan (Pavilion, 2000). Following is a Cherokee tale you might try.

Long ago, the animals of the earth lived in darkness. They heard about a great, glowing sun far away. Each animal wanted to be the one to bring the sun back and place it in the sky. First, the possum tried to wrap the sun around its furry tail. But it was so hot that it burned the fur right off! That is why possums have no fur on their tails. Next, the vulture tried to push the sun into the sky with its head. But the sun burned the feathers off! That is why vultures have bald heads. Only the spider understood that the sun was for everyone, and that all the animals must work together. So she spun a giant web underneath the sun, and stretched it out to all the animals. With a great throw, they bounced the sun all the way up to the sky, where it shines to this day.

BOOK Link

Take children on a journey from dawn to dusk by reading ***Sun Song*** by Jean Marzollo (HarperCollins, 1995). The lilting rhyming verse and breathtaking illustrations show all the things the sun does for people, animals, and plants during a single day, from the moment it rises to the time it sets. The story gently reinforces the cyclical nature of day and night as the book concludes with a brand-new morning.